Nell Hill's
Style at Home

Nell Hill's

Style at Home

Mary Carol Garrity

with Mary Caldwell

Photography by Bryan E. McCay

Andrews McMeel
Publishing

Kansas City

www.andrewsmcmeel.com

Library of Congress Cataloging-in-Publication Data
Garrity, Mary Carol.
   Nell Hill's : style at home / Mary Carol Garrity, with Mary Caldwell : photography by
Bryan E. McCay.--1st U.S. ed.
      p. cm.
   ISBN 0-7407-1874-6
      1. Interior decoration--United States--History--20th century. I. Title: Style at home. II.
Caldwell, Mary. III. Nell Hill's (Shop) IV. Title.

NK2004 .G378 2001
747--dc21

                                                                                        2001022703

10 9 8 7 6 5 4 3 2

Editor: Bruce Shostak
Designer: Alexis Siroc

Produced by Smallwood & Stewart, Inc., New York City

Attention: Schools and Businesses
Andrews McMeel books are available at quantity discounts with bulk purchase for educational,
business, or sales promotional use. For information, please write to: Special Sales Department,
Andrews McMeel Publishing, 4520 Main Street, Kansas City, Missouri 64111.

To my customers,

   who show me style every day

CONTENTS

INTRODUCTION

We do things a bit differently at Nell Hill's, my home furnishings and accessories store in Atchison, Kansas, population 11,000. The store is a study in contradictions. Sophisticated yet unpretentious. Romantic but beautifully practical.

When you call at Nell Hill's, you won't find formal furniture set-ups. Nor will you find out-of-context displays, with pillows shelved on one aisle and tables displayed in another part of the store. Instead, you'll see furniture and accessory groupings that echo real homes, real rooms. Wander from one floor of the store to another and you'll likely come across the same vase used in a dozen entirely different ways. Visit again two weeks later and the whole shop will look new. The one constant is that on any given day, Nell Hill's is packed with merchandise and ideas to help customers make their homes more lively, lovely, and comfortable.

We don't expect you to re-create the look of our showrooms. In fact, we don't expect you to make your home look like anyone else's. Too many people get hung up searching for "style" and fall into the trap of trying to adopt someone else's look. I think it's much more important to outfit your home with things you love and to create an atmosphere that you and your family find accommodating and peaceful. In my own house, I adore being surrounded by beautiful things; I like moving pieces from one room to another, coming up with new ways to display my favorite keepsakes, and switching what's indoors with items that I bring in from the garden. But I also want to feel like I can curl up with a book anywhere in the house. And

I want my guests to know they can plop down and get comfortable in any chair. That's what "style" means to me.

At Nell Hill's, we spend a lot of time talking with people and helping them choose just the right things to take home. Very often visitors bring along photographs of their decorating "trouble spots," and together we come up with some inspired solutions they'll really enjoy. We introduce our customers to a corps of design accents that will bring life to their homes: obelisks and easels, tassels and urns, wall brackets and pedestals, and more. When they return—and it's the rare customer who doesn't call again—we'll talk over what they are happiest with and the new challenges they've begun contemplating. I can tell you that these give-and-take sessions teach me as much as it helps them.

Because I've been lucky enough to "visit" so many homes, to learn so much about how my customers really want to live, and to travel through a world filled with marvelous treasures, I've discovered more than a few tricks to making a home beautiful (even if it means breaking some of those pesky designer rules). That's what I'm setting out to share with you in this book—easy, enjoyable ways to make your home look and feel terrific every day.

Happy decorating!

Mary Carol Garrity

LAYERS AND BACKDROPS

How do I like to decorate a room? Layer by layer,

the way an artist builds up pigments on a canvas, painting a

textured picture that instantly conveys a mood yet has

enough detail to capture your curiosity. My favorite rooms are

comfortable and friendly, lovely and lived-in. And

they break just enough rules and store just enough surprises

that second looks always reveal something new.

At Nell Hill's we set out furnishings and accessories in natural arrangements to evoke the mood of a home. At the same time, the setting is clearly contrived, since our hodgepodge, right, is "over the top" compared with the way most of us really live. Of course, we don't expect your home to be as thickly furnished and accessorized as a showroom—even mine isn't (that's my living room, opposite). We're simply trying to spark ideas. We'd rather let folks envision how a certain lamp will look near an easy chair, on an end table, or in front of a painting. This way, you can start to get an appreciation for the way the layering of individual elements builds up to create a room's total ambience.

In my own living room, I've started with a backdrop of creamy walls, neutral furniture, and area rugs that are all quietly compatible without actually "matching." From there, I've built up layers of interest with books, plates, paintings, and figurines.

The room itself, with its long, narrow shape, lends itself to subdividing. A round table topped with a gracefully arching potted palm, a nice contrast to the room's angular form, splits the room into two distinct areas and serves as a bold backdrop for both. I also employ the tabletop as a constantly changing display area for books and lots of the little accessories that always delight me.

How complex can a room get and still be a comfortable oasis? I say, layer it on. Make it interesting.

When my husband, Dan, and I bought our house, it was divided into a series of dark Victorian rooms. In the living room, our first task was to brighten things up with a backdrop of chamois-colored walls, off-white ceiling, and cream-colored woodwork. With this neutral base, I can easily add or subtract accessories. The colors I like in summer project a different mood from the whites I may add to the room in winter.

Screens do more than hide things. Use them to enhance windows or to soften an expanse of wall or a neglected corner.

Since we virtually live on our screened porch, above, in warm weather, we furnished it with a comfortable daybed and plenty of pillows. I wanted the feeling of relaxing in the garden, so I put up an iron screen — almost a garden gate — and hung botanical prints on it with cotton-twill tape. It introduces another layer without obstructing our view. In the living room, opposite, shutters block glare but don't hide the architectural lines of the window frames the way curtains would. A folding screen transforms a blank corner with a zigzag of drama.

*I'm not one to rearrange furniture often, but I do love
regrouping accessories to strike a new mood in a room.*

I rebel against the notion of lining up objects like so many
ducklings. It's so much more fun to group them in novel ways.
For example, stacks of books, left, make excellent pedestals for
elevating small pieces of china that you want to keep on view.
And how often do you see a candelabra in a vintage dough
board? The grouping appealed to me and seemed in character
with the warm, masculine atmosphere of the study, above.
Who knows? Next time you visit, you might see the candelabra
set on a stack of platters in the dining room, and the dough
board might be serving a few cocktails in the living room.

Be bold. Experiment. Team up several different styles, textures, or materials for a lively yet completely harmonious display.

I believe in regularly seeing fine china and the rest of my "good stuff" rather than locking it away for an all-too-rare special occasion. To keep the mood from becoming stiff and formal, I'll mix and match sets and styles, such as using dinner forks in one pattern and salad forks in another. Inexpensive rattan mats soften the formal edges of a dinner table, opposite, set with majolica, cut crystal, and blown glass. Sometimes I'll create a collection by repeating a single shape in many colors, sizes, or textures, like the balls of wicker, seeds, tiny stones, and rattan, below, that fill an old verdigris bucket.

china closet treasures

*Set some of
your prettiest
plates on
everyday view.*

The mundane contents of some closets are best kept hidden, but china cabinets, open shelving, and glass-fronted cupboards all offer a chance to pair necessary storage with attractive scenery.

- I'm not hung up on the notion that all the dishes must match. I collect different patterns in white and gold, some in small sets but plenty of lone, loved pieces.

- Imagine a country cutting garden. Combine stacks of floral china and majolica, and arrange the groupings like bouquets—whatever pleases your eye or enhances the room is right. Now you'll have cleverly combined elements ready on one shelf.

- Displayed upright, a few matching gold-rimmed platters and a silver one, opposite, make a nice backdrop for stacks of my grandmother's cups and saucers. On easels, the platters are easier to grab than when they're at the bottom of a big, heavy pile.

- In a little nook, above, pretty plates and platters set the stage for a flower display, with coleus leaves in a glass tumbler and hosta blossoms in a champagne flute.

2

3

1

LAYERING PLATES *is a way to put mismatched china to work for more than serving the next meal.* 1 = STACKED PLATTERS *with graduated but disparate outlines and a graceful footed dish lift a bedside alarm clock just to pillow level.* 2 = A TABLETOP BLOSSOM *of complementary painted and transferware plates showcases a floral porcelain box.* 3 = A PLATE PLATFORM *on a wirework table provides secure display space for a little easel and print.*

*The heart of almost every home, the kitchen can be just
as personalized and pretty as the rest of the house.*

I lived with the previous owner's turquoise kitchen for so long that it was a real relief when we redid the room in soothing tones of gray, sage, and cream. I don't like a kitchen that's fussy, but there are ways to make what could be ordinary more appealing. Keeping gleaming bouquets of cutlery in vases, above, means I never have to go rooting around in a silverware drawer. A large platter behind the faucet, opposite, works as a beautiful and easily cleaned backsplash. A cake stand proves ideal for keeping soap high and dry above puddles but still handy.

Reconsider what makes a good backdrop for any piece of furniture, and you may just solve a puzzling floor plan.

Multiple doorways in a bedroom are necessities if they lead to lots of closets and a bath en suite — but they can make it difficult to position a queen-size bed. When I started to think of two windows as a light-filled headboard, on the other hand, the floor plan suddenly made sense. The moldings between our windows even offered a good spot for the accent I like most in the room: a small convex mirror. A chair placed at bedside catches the inevitable overflow from my table.

SETTING STILL LIFES

Personalize a room with a tableau of favorite

things. Walls, furniture, carpets — they all contribute

style and comfort. But without that gilding of special objects,

rooms can feel so stark and impersonal. Souvenirs, keepsakes,

family mementos, and costly antiques all belong together.

Tell a story. Make the arrangements as interesting

as what's on show. Then rearrange it all.

Much of the fun I have at work is helping customers select accessories that will personalize their homes. I'm fascinated with how easy it is to change a look by adding or subtracting an object or two. At our stores, we have the luxury of working with a constant influx of new merchandise, so we invent new displays almost daily.

Of course, you probably won't want to rearrange so often at home, but you can make changes to reflect your moods or the seasons. Forget about those perfectly symmetrical, not-a-hair-out-of-place shots you see in magazines. Forget flavor-of-the-moment fashion. Surround yourself with what you like to look at, things that say "home" to you.

Don't think you need to have items lined up in a curio cabinet or have only one big object right in the center of a table. Often, a cluster—a still life—looks best, revealing a new feature each time it's examined. Setting a figurine on a stack of books or on another pedestal brings height to a display, making the tableau more dynamic. A bouquet of feathers in an urn, opposite, draws the eye upward even further. I sometimes corral collections on trays or cake stands, or fence in objects with a stack of hardcover books, above, to create a niche. Whatever suits your taste, remember that displays of treasured belongings reflect your personality and talents.

*Strength in numbers: A chorus
of small objects has greater impact
than a solo display.*

Diminutive treasures are often overlooked
when scattered here and there. Grouped
together, they bring life to an end table or
double for a bouquet on a sideboard. These
vases look like family heirlooms, but they're
all new and inexpensive. Several pieces
of antique transferware nearby provide
contrast. The irreverently inverted saucer is
a shapely pedestal for one of the vases.

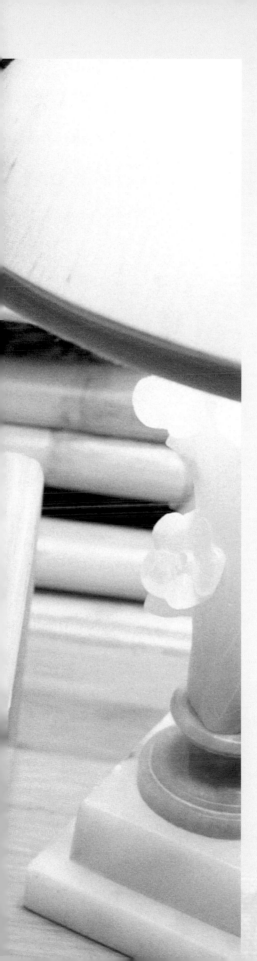

Tell stories: They are as fun to create as they are to see,
and bring a lovely resonance into your home.

In the powder room tucked beneath our entryway stairs, there's just enough space for a piece of delicate furniture. Our bamboo vanity, left, provides attractive storage as well as a surface for a few special things. I like the silver rose that seems to have fallen from the bouquet of real roses above it. In the living room, a painted metal bird, above, wades in a silver dish set on a suitably titled book, the kind of playful pairing that elicits a chuckle once a visitor makes the connection.

CONSTANT EVOLUTION

best describes the still lifes on my foyer table.

1 - LOOSE GROUPINGS like this one satisfy my penchant for informality. The glass cloches lend unrelated elements a unified look.

2 - A WEIGHTIER VERSION includes larger objects and dashes of red. 3 - THE MORE FORMAL COMPOSITION—symmetrical but definitely not stiff—works well to set a mood for an evening party, with silvered glass to reflect and multiply the candlelight.

Mingle metals. A still life that pairs silver and brass or bronze and rusted iron has more character than a mono-metallic scheme.

People are sometimes intimidated by the idea of letting a formal piece of silver keep company with an iron urn carried in from the garden, but the contrast is pleasing. Arranged on a small table between doorways, this three-dimensional vignette, below is a refreshing change of pace from a flat, framed picture in that spot. A library table, opposite, offers space for an even more idiosyncratic grouping of formal urns, a clock, and porcelain mixed in with such whimsical touches as feathers, a leather valise, and a finial.

Consider an object's intended purpose, then challenge yourself to dream up other, totally unconnected treatments.

Instead of setting two iron lovebirds at military attention side by side on the tabletop, opposite, I propped one up on a couple of books so it looks as if he's wooing his mate in front of a garden gate. I think of the Wardian case, really designed as a miniature greenhouse, as a portable curio cabinet. As shown, above, it holds transferware teacups, but a few days later, it's just as likely to be home to the lovebirds at left, a cow creamer, or even a potted violet or two.

the great out-of-drawers

Consider vintage silverware as lovely palm-size sculptures.

We see sets of flatware so often that we sometimes overlook each piece's intrinsic beauty, the variety of shapes and styles of handles, and the contrast of round bowl, pointed tines, and mirror-like blades. Good-looking utensils definitely deserve a showing beyond their utilitarian appearance at mealtime, so don't keep them a secret in the sideboard drawers.

- Vintage silver oyster forks and mother-of-pearl-handled knives fanned out in a semi-circle, opposite, suggest the lines of a sundial; a magnifying glass echoes the pattern.

- I keep a four-piece hors d'oeuvres set, the handles sporting an Oriental design, near the edge of my living room's center table, above. The books form a border that contains the utensils visually.

- A "bouquet" of utensils in a glass jar or vase is handy in the kitchen, and also looks pretty on a mantel or catching sunlight on a windowsill. This treatment works with other similarly shaped objects, too, such as writing implements, letter openers, pen knives, or antique crochet and button hooks.

*Pedestals, whether they are carved platforms designed
for just that purpose or makeshift stacks of books, adjust
the sizes of objects and give everything more dimension.*

Why not put everyone on a pedestal? For a fancy lineup on
a sideboard, right, those inexpensive round wood pedestals
available at import stores unify a teacup and a silver service
with two Chinese-style lamps mounted on carved bases. The
rose bouquet gets a gleaming lift from a mirrored plateau, while
the platters and the round mirror float on wooden easels. In
a less structured scene, above, books piled to various heights
support terraced arrangements of objects and framed photographs. Antique boxes or other cases would also do the job.

Tiered dessert stands, pretty in their own right, perform like miniature etageres, elevating dainty pieces.

Don't think you can't display inexpensive or purely sentimental items alongside more "legitimate" collectibles. Every time I see a certain little round metal box, with its old coins, I'm reminded of my maternal grandmother, Nell Hill, and her stories of playing with the tin as a child bumping along dusty roads in a covered wagon. To me, it's every bit as precious as the exquisite porcelain and silver boxes around it. The contrast, I think, makes the whole arrangement far more intriguing.

ODD PIECES OF GLASS, *from paperweights and florist's marbles to faceted cut crystal, can be gathered into stunning center-pieces. The idea is quite easy—begin with a hunt around the house for the elements.* 1 ▪ OLD BOTTLES, *pearlescent with age, contrast with the clear glass of two cake stands.* 2 ▪ ORPHANED DECANTER STOPPERS *become icy diamonds in a compote.* 3 ▪ A VASE *doesn't need flowers when it's accompanied by complementary glass vessels.*

FABRIC MOODS

Soft furnishings — curtains, pillows, throws,

and more — can sway the mood of a room from

casual to chic, from sunny to sedate.

If you want to update a room without investing in

new furniture or undertaking elaborate

renovations to floors and walls, look to fabric

for a wealth of solutions.

As testimony to my fondness for all kinds of fabric, I opened a second store in Atchison, Kansas. G. Diebolts, named for my late father, specializes in custom bedding, linens, and decorative accessories for the bedroom. But that's another story.

It might be just because I have ready access to so many wonderful materials, but I frequently find myself longing to bring new fabrics into my home. With the backdrop of neutral furnishings as the starting point, it's relatively easy to get a fresh, pulled-together look by swapping out cushions or a throw for the sofa, above. And while a love seat or an easy chair completely dressed in a brilliant print would probably be too loud for my taste, accent fabrics allow me to be bold in small doses that don't overwhelm the room.

My penchant for mixing casual and formal extends to fabrics, too. In choosing pillows for the sofa, for example, I might opt for three fabrics in related colors that each feel different to the touch. Varying patterns — such as the plaid, paisley, and floral, opposite — work if they share a palette or density of color. But even if fabrics are fine needlepoints or formal brocades, I still want them to look as if I could go and pounce on them — something my cats like to do just before they curl up for a nap.

As long as fabrics don't fight each other, it's fine to go for odd pairings that might not always seem to be a match.

The living room, left, in the home of my friends Marilyn and John Buehler shows how fabrics can keep a neutral color scheme from becoming too austere. Toile seats and pillows in black and white—usually a stark pairing in contemporary design—and sheer scrim hung at the windows keep the overall feeling here pretty and serene; a transferware platter fits right in. For a warmer mood, above, a tapestry ottoman meets a cinnamon-striped chair. They don't actually coordinate, but they certainly don't clash; they create an engaging complexity.

Textured materials like wicker, bamboo, and velvet invigorate rooms that have limited color palettes.

My friends Ann and Guy Humphreys chose cream cotton upholstery and an immense jacket-leather ottoman for their living room. With this neutral backdrop, Ann can easily transform the look of the room by slipping new covers on the pillows and changing the throw on the sofa. Underfoot, a sea grass rug brings more texture. These natural woven rugs help keep rooms from seeming too fancy. And because many are relatively inexpensive, particularly those made of coir, you don't need to live with them forever to feel you've got your money's worth.

2

3

1

FRESHEN A SOFA with a change of pillows. Start with good inserts (I prefer down), then switch covers, usually with modest cost and effort. To double the options, select different fabrics for the front and back of each pillow. 1 - AN OVERSIZE SQUARE seduces afternoon nappers. 2 - OPULENT FABRICS with trims and tassels complement a chenille throw. 3 - BED PILLOWS in plump button-closure cases are cozy stand-ins for the sofa's original trio of back cushions.

Play up — don't cover up — a window's beauty and all that natural light with less-is-more textile treatments.

To maximize daylight yet not have completely bare windows, try a trick from architect Reed Graves and his wife, Brenda. Sew a casing across the center of a folded triangle of fabric (a large linen napkin is good) and slip it over a tension rod. The result, above, is a simple valance that suggests an inverted architectural pediment. Sew a tassel at the bottom for weight and flourish. Instead of hanging heavy, old-fashioned drapery, Marilyn Buehler swags lengths of inexpensive scrim over brass hooks at the corners of the window frames, opposite.

sheer simplicity

Set a romantic mood by draping the gauziest of fabrics.

Scrim, a loosely woven cotton fabric priced at just a few dollars a yard, has to be one of the best bargains in home decorating. It's easily draped and gathered—no sewing required—to bring romantic refinement or soft enchantment to any room.

- I transformed a freestanding bathtub, above, into an ethereal tented retreat by pulling lengths of scrim through a crown-shaped bracket mounted on the wall. As a bonus, the fabric concealed a damaged portion of my antique mirror's frame.

- In a bedroom, a similar treatment can substitute for a headboard or a four-poster canopy. To make it more opulent, braid lengths of scrim a short distance out from the bracket, then let the lengths puddle on the floor; tuck under the raw edges.

- For summer entertaining out of doors, I love to drape scrim as garlands between tree branches, over picnic tables, and around the screened walls of my porch. When breezes waft in, the scrim floats about like wispy clouds.

For guest rooms, muted colors and soothing fabrics help give each visitor a night of peaceful rest.

In a room suffused with browns and golds, a floral quilt and striped curtains introduce just the right degree of pattern; the robin's egg blue on the walls holds the elements together. I love folding back the sheets and covers and piling up the pillows to reveal all the contrasting fabrics—those slightly rumpled bedclothes always look so inviting. Fringed throw pillows work as long as they pick up the colors of the bedding.

Walls and Pictures

Most walls in a house may well be flat, but
what you choose to display on them doesn't have
to be. Hanging framed art is just the start of
a long list of ways to make your walls flower.
Build outward, but don't forget the useful niches
in bookcases. Embrace tradition, but try an
offbeat arrangement. Redefine eye level.

A flat interior wall, to my eye, is a stimulating sight indeed, a blank slate offering almost unlimited opportunities to liven up the room.

I'm not averse to having framed pictures on the wall—my home is full of them—but centering a single "important" painting over a table or sofa, or symmetrically aligning a pair of botanical prints above the fireplace, is not exactly my idea of satisfaction. I'm much more likely to come up with quirky little groupings like the one shown above, with some in out-of-the-way or overlooked spots. I might prop frames atop a wall bracket or wood molding for more architectural interest.

In my experience, people too often worry as much about coordinating frames as they do about grouping the artwork they surround. Relax. It's okay to assemble an arrangement that includes silver and gold frames, or wood and painted porcelain. In fact, I prefer the mix. Proportion should be considered, however, so that the artwork on the walls neither overwhelms the room nor gets lost.

Finally, I interpret the notion of "wall" a little loosely—bookcases, opposite, or glass-fronted cabinets, doors, and windows are really just extensions of walls. So they're fair game for displaying framed art, photographs, even monograms from beloved antique linens that have become too shabby to use.

THE MIRROR *in my entryway has an ornate gilt frame, but that doesn't limit how I accessorize the space.* 1 = BOTANICAL PRINTS *and plates emphasize the floral curves of the frame itself.* 2 = CLASSICALLY INSPIRED *objects and prints create an antiquarian feeling that is more masculine.* 3 = PICTURES OF FROGS *and pieces of new majolica create a lighthearted summertime scene; wicker balls atop white candlesticks replace the lamps.*

Take advantage of long, unbroken expanses and of tight spaces alike. Create more architecture with pairs of pictures or a great big suite of them.

I got a kick out of pairing flora and fauna in the dining room, left, with Limoges trout plates swimming over the botanicals. From a design standpoint, the round plates add a welcome contrast to the rectangular prints, and the gold picture ledges keep the plates from looking as if they're drifting. On another side of the room, above, antique prints of Henry Knox and Richard Montgomery, Revolutionary War generals, nicely fill the slice of wall between a door and a window.

Think of doorways as opportunities, not obstacles, when planning how to arrange framed art.

In our grass-cloth-walled study, above, Dan and I decided to break up the expected pairings of pictures. Our solution was to hang them bordered on one side by the doorway in a dense configuration that has a sweep of upward movement — one picture looks like as if it is climbing over the top. My friends Marilyn and John Buehler exhibit pictures on the infrequently opened doors of a storage closet, right, at one end of their dining room. The walls remain bare.

Custom dictates hanging artwork at eye level. Why? I prefer to put the whole room into decorative play.

When someone visits a room I've had anything to do with, it usually takes a while to drink in the whole scene. The window-seat alcove in my living room, opposite, even the lofty bit near the ceiling, is an inviting gallery for butterflies (the one that didn't fit "flew" to another spot in the room) and botanicals. Similarly, I hung an engraving in that normally bare spot over a door, above, that leads to the screened porch.

*Framed art needn't be confined to being hung on a wall. I love
to prop it against any surface that's secure enough to hold it.*

By conceiving temporary displays, such as the shell print resting against a
window of our guest room, below, you can present miscellaneous pictures
that might not have a perfect home on the wall. In my living room, I've
treated a bookcase, opposite, as an extension of the wall to show off a
collection of mounted butterflies. It's easy to rearrange them because they're
not hung from hooks nailed to the wall. With little effort I can move the
biggest box of butterflies to the top, or arrange them on the diagonal.

a shelf with a view

Make shelves of open storage as artistic as they are convenient.

Cubbyholes in a bedroom or home office, like glass-fronted cabinets in a kitchen, are practical, but they do demand careful consideration of what's kept within.

- Fold and stack attractive out-of-season quilts, blankets, or even sweaters and enjoy the striped effect of their patterns and textures while they're not in use.

- Store smaller linens — extra washcloths, bed sheets, pillowcases — that don't fit anywhere else in handsome storage baskets.

- Create intriguing contrasts of materials. Cover up anything that you don't want on view by tacking a pretty scarf or a fabric square over one shelf.

- Designate a shelf or two for strictly decorative purposes. Consider it as an open memory box, full of favorite mementos from a trip or a treasured experience.

WALL BRACKETS *make shapely ledges*

for displaying pictures, as well as for daily use.

1 ∞ AN ORNATE BRACKET *made of economical*

molded resin holds soap, compensating for the

lack of space on a pedestal sink. 2 ∞ A SLICE

OF WALL *between a kitchen doorway and a book-*

case is just wide enough for a winsome grouping

of bracket, majolica creamer, and antique print.

3 ∞ WAIST-HIGH *in an entryway, a bracket is*

always ready to catch house keys or mail.

BUTTERFLIES   MARCUS SCHNECK

KEN
DRUSE   THE   NATURAL GARDEN

*A mantel is really just an extension of the wall, a ledge
perfectly designed for leaning mirrors or pictures and creating
ever-changing displays of whatever pleases your eye.*

Rather than hang a picture dead-center over the fireplace, Brenda
Graves leaned a painting in place toward one end of the mantel, above,
balanced by an undulating wave of plates on easels. She's the third-
generation owner of a fabulous plate collection, and the mantel allows
her to rotate favorites frequently. Even without stately tapers, a silver
candelabra, opposite, can be appreciated for its graceful form; another
candlestick makes a pedestal for a garden bouquet in a mint julep cup.

Consider balance and pleasing proportions, not metronomic mirror images, when decorating walls, mantels, and fireplaces.

Architectural elements such as the iron grate on Ann Humphreys's mantel are a good way to introduce drama to a room's vertical plane. Picking up the design of the fire screen without repeating it exactly, the grate is centered above the hearth; it's flanked by a clock and a candelabra and fronted with a glass tray and binoculars for a look that's anything but stiff. Pairs of pictures on either side of the fireplace provide just enough perfect symmetry.

Look up! The top of an armoire and the space above a door-way offer unique stages for fragile and heavy objects alike.

Instead of mounting a coat and hat rack in the back entryway, only to be buried under outerware, I hung it over a doorway, above, where its clean lines can be admired and its purpose redirected as light fixture-cum-display ledge. (Make sure these objects won't knock anyone in the head.) In our guest bedroom, right, a serene bust keeps watch. I like the way she brings the decorating scheme out from the wall, yet I've made sure not to clutter the top with anything else but the large framed print.

ROMANCING THE HOME

There's a special pleasure that comes with sharing

your home with guests. A sign of welcome at the entrance,

visual treats throughout the house, artful accessories

that sparkle or glow in candlelight — these are the

touches that make your house inviting and uniquely yours.

There is, in truth, no place like home.

A pleasing and peaceful refuge is what I crave after the delightful craziness of my working hours. Having that at home is a must. Another must is making guests feel welcome and at ease. Starting at the entrance, moving through the house, and drifting out to the screened porch and terrace, I introduce special notes of romance, magic, and drama. It's so important to set the stage.

If the front door is the face of a house, you need to provide its expression. I love flowers, but quite honestly I'm not at my best digging in the dirt, so my walkway is lined with plants in urns and pots rather than with meticulously tended beds. And I love the fact that potted plants can be arranged and rearranged.

On the door itself I hang a flower basket planted with hardy fellows like geraniums and ivy. It sprouts all summer, asking only for a periodic drink of water. Before a party, I might loop a length of scrim or a silk scarf through the door knocker.

Look around and see what you can put to use. A branch from a shrub in need of pruning brings an empty urn to life, opposite; stems of coleus, above, fill a vase if flowers are scarce. So much around the house can be adapted, so let your imagination loose. Step through the front door, and I'll show you a few of my favorite ideas for setting the stage.

*Entertaining at sundown is
unthinkable without the soft glow
of candles and lanterns.*

On warm-weather evenings, votives flicker
from a simple metal chandelier on my
screened porch. Along with more votives in
little flowerpots on the railing, some tapers
here and there, and a fat pillar atop a cast-
metal urn, they provide all the light we need
when friends stop by for a glass of wine.
Always have three or four kinds of candles
stocked in your pantry, and be flexible with
what you choose to use as a candleholder;
the decorative possibilities are limitless.

See what's on hand and you'll probably find everything you need for making lovely centerpieces or table accents.

If you have a dreamed-of cutting garden, skip this page and head outside for an armful of blossoms. But if you're like me — with a less-than-green thumb and little desire to be running off to the florist for expensive arrangements — look around for containers you already own to dress up the table. Two arrangements I like every time: several white roses tucked into a creamer, above, and vibrant limes piled in an urn, opposite, paired with a lemon-lidded sugar bowl.

GARDEN URNS, *splashy decorative objects to begin with, are terrific showmen, able to present anything with flair.* 1 = A TOMATO PYRAMID *displays the vegetable garden's baubles for a day or two before it's time for the salad bowl.* 2 = THREE TAPERS *fit snugly into a diminutive urn and become a triple-wicked pillar candle; springy sphagnum moss fills the gaps.* 3 = NAPKINS AND SILVER *are bunched like a bouquet for an outdoor buffet.*

The miracle of glass is that it simultaneously contains and reveals, so match the right clear vase to the arrangement.

Pretty is as pretty does, many a grandmother has been heard to say; that's what I think of with my cutlery displayed in a celery vase, above. The glass and silver catch sunbeams and send light dancing, and yet it's supremely handy storage, too. With a collection of tall slender glass vases, opposite, a few stems of graceful, leggy flowers dress up beautifully without blocking light at a window or, on a dinner table, inhibiting views from guest to guest.

Conjure some unexpected charm at an outdoor party by playing with favorite objects you typically keep indoors.

I'm crazy for pretty plates, so I love to come up with as many ways to use them as possible. For a little party on the front terrace, I went dish gathering and chose a mostly pink and green theme. Propped in cup and saucer holders, the plates add an especially lovely border around the terrace rail and reflect the candles (in lieu of teacups) once the sun goes down. I layered some, like the round plate and the small metal leaf. And I adore the two frogs — one is pictured on a plate, the other is the vase next to the wine bottles — so perfect for the garden setting.

2

3

1

PLAY WITH FIRE *and you can create so many reflective effects. It's all in the math: adding and subtracting.* 1 = AN EMPTY HEARTH *in summer can still glow, but with candlelight. Rather than place pillars in the firebox, we put them on pedestals so they would also illuminate the mantel.* 2 = GLASS ORBS *interspersed with tea lights dress the mantel for a party.* 3 = TWO JASMINE BLOSSOMS *in an amber globe vase add a delicate touch.*

luxury every day

*Celebrate
with your best,
and do so as
often as possible.*

Crystal, china, silver — all are meant to be enjoyed, so don't wait for a formal occasion. Display
your favorites and see them every day. And if you have a chance to unwind over a quiet dinner
for two at home, set the table as if you were expecting honored guests, because you are.

- Don't wait for company. Bring out something to make every meal elegant.

- It is a luxury to sit down to dinner in a room where we don't normally eat. In my
  living room, I cleared the always laden center table. Then I unfolded a pretty toile
  duvet cover and pressed it into service as a tablecloth. I positioned a candelabra and
  silver-plated birds — I was inspired by the pattern of the toile — and was ready for,
  I confess, takeout food.

- The dining room is mostly a single-purpose room, so it is the perfect place to pull
  out all the stops. My friend Brenda Graves made a luxurious arrangement of her
  heirloom silver and crystal, on the following pages, on the sideboard in her dining
  room. Luscious pink roses have just enough color without taking center stage.

PORTFOLIO

Here are a few of my golden rules
of design. They reflect my
answers to the questions most frequently
asked by visitors to Nell Hill's.

ROOM BY ROOM

*A*ttitudes about functions and furnishings evolve, and rooms that were considered "private" generations ago — the kitchen, a sewing room, even the bedroom — are now comfortably opened to guests every day. The front parlor (and Atchison had a great many of them) was set aside for the most formal, special visits. The furniture lasted a lifetime, partly because it was so seldom used. Now the front parlor has become a living room, and many of us have family rooms, libraries, breakfast rooms, bedroom suites, even fantasy bathrooms. In some homes, the dining room must do double duty as a home office; the laundry room as a pantry; the living room as a homework center. But it's still safe to say that each part of the house gets assigned its own purpose (or purposes) and, with it, its own flow and style.

Whether I've lived in a studio or a cottage or the house I'm in now, practicality has always been all-important: I can't run my life if I can't find my car keys, and no matter how pretty my platters are, my dinner party's not a success if the food is two hours late. But once the necessities have been taken care of, I like to start throwing a few curves. My kitchen doesn't have to be a shrine to food preparation, and I wouldn't feel inspired there without framed prints on the walls, soft lighting for thumbing through cookbooks, and whimsies like my Wardian case with its ever-changing tableaux. Here are some of my theories about room-by-room decorating.

The ENTRYWAY introduces visitors to your home. If the front door is the main entry for a large family, get oversize decorative baskets

or a pretty armoire to collect outerwear and gear. As far as design goes, you can go for sparse drama, such as leaning a huge mirror on the floor; you can jazz the foyer up with an exuberant display. Whichever approach you choose, make sure that people can walk through comfortably. A bench or an easy chair just inside the door is a convenient spot to pull off boots or set down packages. A long entry is a good spot for a gallery of favorite items like wall pockets. One treatment I like is a shallow iron baker's rack set with exquisite pieces of porcelain.

I think the most important consideration for any LIVING ROOM is comfortable seating to encourage congenial chats. How you achieve this depends on the proportions of the room. Even in small rooms, my instinct is to keep sofas and chairs away from the walls, facing each other to encourage intimacy. I love tables behind sofas and dress them with plants, statuary, books — anything to create a backdrop. In my own long living room, I have set up two separate conversation areas, divided physically and visually by a good-size pedestal table that acts as a changing display for many of my favorite things. It might be an urn or a myrtle topiary, a few cast-iron animals, or stacks of new and antiquarian books to suit the season at hand.

In many houses, the DINING ROOM is the most formal, and least used, room. I make a conscious effort to inject a note of humor or surprise here, and I change the display at least seasonally. Instead of the predictable centerpiece of candles and flowers, I'm likely to set a gazing ball on a pedestal from the garden or group three glass cloches with something different under each — say, a potted plant, a cast-iron figurine, and a china teacup. Once, I lugged in a small birdbath and planted it with pansies as a centerpiece.

Some people expect a KITCHEN to be all business: food storage and preparation, family message center, homework station. I agree that the layout should be efficient, but there's still plenty of leeway for decorative surprise. I like mixing in formal pieces and "good" china among the everyday cookware and utensils. I also commandeer pieces or containers that would normally be kept elsewhere in the house but go a long way toward organizing life and work in the kitchen. A little footed silver tray, for example, collects containers of our first-aid supplies and the like, while a cast-iron planter holds cooking oils, vinegars, and whatever wine we're drinking that week. Dish towels, rolled up and stored in a wire basket, are attractive and ready for action. I prefer to stash the toaster and the food processor — any small appliance I don't use daily — in a drawer or a cupboard.

In a home LIBRARY, ergonomics and beauty can coexist peacefully. Your computer does not have to be concealed in an antique armoire. But forget the ugly laminate work station and set up your system on an interesting table. Make the workspace convenient and functional, and high-tech equipment can mingle comfortably with the rest of the room. Keep more prosaic desktop items such as pens, floppy disks or CDs, and postage attractively corralled in baskets or boxes.

Outfit your room with good lamps, comfy chairs, a plump ottoman, and some sturdy shelves. Allow space on the shelves for lamps, and finish the shelf edges with trim or molding. Then surround yourself with books and things you love. However utilitarian the bookcase, it can also serve as a gallery for photos, art, and collectibles. I hung a mirror on the bookcase in our library — it really helps open up the small room.

Because it's the least public area in the home, the BEDROOM often has last priority where decorating is concerned. It's so pleasant, however, to wake up in a peaceful, personal space, that I recommend making bedrooms into sanctuaries. If your nightstand isn't big enough to hold everything you want, park a chair, a wooden trunk, or a large basket beside to collect potential clutter. Set a favorite photograph next to the reading lamp.

Children's bedrooms have to be rethought almost as often as the kids outgrow their shoes. Beyond bed and dresser, add easy storage — wicker baskets for laundry, canvas-sided carts for sports gear, tin beach pails for paintbrushes or markers. Then step back and let your child indulge in self-expression with posters and everything else.

For a guest bedroom, emphasize privacy and comfort, and try to anticipate anything that a guest might need. I'll set out a basket with a couple of thick towels, a face cloth, and sample-size bottles of shampoo and other toiletries. When we have visitors, I put out a couple of current magazines; when close friends come to stay, I know their taste in books and choose one or two from my library for them. On the nightstand, it's nice to put a water pitcher and a jar with cookies or some fresh fruit. I let guests know that they can expect to find a carafe of fresh coffee outside the door in the morning, so they can enjoy that first wake-up cup in peace.

Decorating the BATHROOM may be trickier than decorating most other rooms, especially when you consider that space is often

cramped and necessary but large, unattractive products abound. So while you can set the mood of the room with color, reconcile comfort, function, and style by keeping must-haves contained but

handy. I have a large apothecary jar for a ready supply of cotton balls, and lots of handsome boxes to hold mundane items such as cosmetics, hair rollers, patent medicines, and the like. Garden workbaskets or vintage wire bins can hold generous supplies of towels or extra toilet paper. If you have room, supplement a conventional vanity with a bedroom nightstand or a small wooden bureau.

Do you have a TERRACE? Entertaining there need not be a cliché of plastic supplies meant only for outdoor use. On even a casual evening, I'll create a magical but temporary ambience. I've been known to take upholstered chairs, silver, candlesticks, and stemware outdoors. They come as a delightful surprise and show guests that you've gone out of your way to make the gathering special. The most rustic, ordinary picnic tables and deck chairs can easily be dressed up with floats of scrim. On any good-weather day, your best vintage linens sparkle in the sun as table covers or improvised awnings for dappled shade. Natural seasonal items—budding branches in spring, flowers or vegetables in summer, acorns or colorful leaves in fall—can be gathered into a basket, an urn, or a clay flowerpot for instant decorating.

My Faithful Foot Soldiers

So often visitors to Nell Hill's bring along photographs of their houses, and we'll sit down together to talk about how to "make it beautiful." In the photos, I see nicely proportioned living rooms with good sofas and chairs, a few lamps and side tables, maybe an area rug, and usually some prints on the wall. Perhaps the dining room boasts a handsome table and sideboard with stately straight-backed chairs and a graceful chandelier. A bedroom features a bed, dressers, an armoire or a chest, mirrors, and bedside tables. In short, everything that has been chosen is fine, but still, there's something missing.

What's missing are the finishing touches that express personality, fill the rooms with life, intrigue guests, and amuse the family. Like the fragrance in a rose, spirit makes the room. I know it's time to call on my faithful foot soldiers, my hardy band of decorative elements that bring distinction to a table or the mantel, that move gracefully from living room to bedroom as the mood strikes, and that serve as foundations for seasonal decorations. Here are my ten favorites.

Tassels

A simple tassel — perhaps a stylized descendant of a frayed rope? — can give a quick lift to diverse furnishings and accessories. Once used mainly as tiebacks for formal curtains, tassels now show up in any room of the home and include casual styles made of jute and multicolored cotton as well as traditional "heavy" examples of silk, sometimes combined with porcelain or wooden beads. I like the way tassels change the look of a floor lamp, for instance, when looped around the shade or the base. They can be gorgeous tied around candlesticks or chair backs, or as an accent for a throw pillow, a cabinet knob, the handle of a pitcher, or a curtain rod finial. Tie a tiny tassel to the key of an armoire or a china cabinet, or to the handle of a sugar bowl or a creamer.

Urns

You can't have too many urns. You'll find them in concrete and cast iron, porcelain and pottery, silver and fiberglass. I love that their robust silhouettes are so classical, so traditional — and yet new urns come in so many shapes, colors, and sizes at so many prices that there are urns for every house. An urn is great all alone — try an oversize one by your front door, filled with dried hydrangea, cattails, or evergreen branches. Group a bunch of small, empty urns made of different materials to form a mantel display. For a dinner-table center-piece, set a pot of ivy or a dozen oranges and apples in a porcelain or pottery urn. Effective organizers, urns hold makeup brushes on a dressing table, silverware in the kitchen, or pens and pencils in your study.

EASELS

Another Nell Hill's staple, easels range from small — two or three inches high, sized for propping up a saucer or a framed photo — to tall, five feet or more, perfect for a large framed painting, a print, or a mirror. Since you don't have to deal with hooks in the wall, easels make it easy to switch what is on display, as the season or your mood changes. The easels I like are usually made of iron or wood. At their most basic, they are functional and unobtrusive, but some are so decorative that they too can become part of the display. Instead of a predictable arrangement of a silver tea service on its own tray, I like to prop the tray on an easel and have it act as a backdrop for the rest of the service.

BOOKS

Books are important to me, mostly because I want to have the kind of comfortable home where I and everyone else can curl up almost anywhere and read. I also believe they are really effective, yet usually overlooked, as decorating tools. Often, I flout conventional wisdom about not separating books and their covers (I keep the jackets in a safe place until it's time to put them back on the books), and have fun stacking up volumes with binding colors that complement or match a still life of favorite objects. Or I'll choose a book with a title on the spine that playfully comments on the displayed objects. I like books as decorative pillars and props, too. A stack of them can be a fully adjustable pedestal for so many things.

GLASS

Like the basic black dress of fashion fame, glass goes with everything. The shapes are infinite: bowls, vases, urns, balls, curios, sculpture. Put glass near a window and it catches the sunlight, sometimes refracting the rays into a rainbow across a wall or a tabletop. A few clear-glass pieces mixed in with opaque containers can keep the group from appearing too heavy. Flowers and candles are naturals, but you can easily change the look of a glass container by filling it with Christmas balls, marbles, buttons, seashells, jewelry—you name it. Team glass with silver for elegance; the shimmer and shine volley to and fro beautifully. Mercury glass and colored glass objects are fun, too; I adore gazing balls, and think they are underrated as decorations.

SCREENS

Picture a vintage movie scene, with the heroine changing her outfit behind a folding screen. A screen can be equally provocative at home, as a decorating device. It can conceal things you'd rather not reveal—great clutter cover—or simply perk up a blah corner of a room. I've had everything from an old iron screen on the porch to an antique screen on a staircase half-landing. I've found some unconventional functions for screens, too: as a headboard for a bed and as a backdrop for a buffet instead of the expected mirror or painting. Tabletop screens anchor a display; short screens work well in smaller, low-ceilinged rooms. A charming old screen that's too rickety to be trusted on its feet can be flattened and mounted on the wall as art. Outdoors, wire screens keep cooking equipment and lounge chairs happily oblivious of each other.

PILLOWS

Pillows are my absolute
favorite accessories, pairing
two of my top decorating criteria: comfort and
style. It's impossible to have too many — soft,
squishy pillows for bed and reading chairs, oversize floor pillows (always grabbed by my friends
who like to sit on the floor around the food-
laden coffee table), small bolsters and cushions
to put behind your back on the sofa. Underscore
the coziness of a family room with denim pillow
covers; tone down formality in the living room
with pillows in a "crossover" fabric such as
corduroy or wool flannel. Recently, I've seen
pillows covered with pieces of vintage sweaters.
You can mix and match pillow covers in bolder
combinations than you would for upholstery,
because when you tire of a look, it's inexpensive
to just replace the covers.

PLATTERS

I know some people think
of platters merely as utilitarian
food servers — basically overgrown plates.
To me, however, they are individual pieces of
art, ready to enhance the mood of a room, and I
cherish my diverse collection of one-of-a-kind
(yes, what others might consider mismatched)
platters. I love platters hanging on the wall,
displayed on an easel, or set on an end table as
a base for a lamp or to underline an object that's
deserving of special notice. I'll group pillar
candles on one of my gold-rimmed platters and
adore the glow. A platter in my bedroom holds
half a dozen strings of old pearls. One of my
favorite platters is fairly deep, and in the winter
I fill it with stones and force hyacinths in it. If a
platter is pretty, it doesn't matter to me whether
it has a chip or a crazed surface; honorable signs
of wear only suggest its interesting past.

SIDE CHAIRS

I get so excited when I come across an old wooden side chair. Many of them are like pieces of art, with beautifully proportioned backs and graceful legs. Once you've got a few in your home, I think you'll find them pretty indispensable, too. I never bother about the size of the chair: a tall one, almost as high as a stool, holds a stack of the cookbooks I'll be working from for a party. In the bedroom, overflow from my night table is still handy. On the chair in my guest room, a fluffy blanket and three fat pillows offer themselves to make a visitor's bed just right. Even children's side chairs — *especially* children's side chairs — are terrific helpers. In the bathroom, I can keep a supply of folded towels stacked low and out of the way on one; in the living room, a pair of side chairs support stacks of art books and heavy design magazines.

TRAYS

Years ago, every home had a tea tray, elegant, of course, but strong enough to carry the tea service and plates of sandwiches out to guests. I'm still infatuated with trays and can honestly say that I've never met one I couldn't do something with. Silver trays are terrific lined up on wall brackets; they certainly don't have to match. Wooden trays serve as the stages for many of my rustic still lifes, the ones that feature bird's nests and tiny birdhouses. An oversize tray with legs holds everything I need for correspondence so that I can get right to work whenever I find time for a few quick notes. And my hands-down favorite trays are the two that live in my bedroom and bathroom: Sunday newspapers with breakfast in bed and a tray across the tub with a mirror, a body brush, a book, and a glass of wine: What more could anyone ask?

Lists I Can't Resist

7 Rules

to Break *I hate rules, especially those dreamed up by people who live in houses that look like showrooms. Here are some decorating myths you can happily ignore:*

Myth #1 Choose one style and make sure all your furnishings and accessories fit with the theme.

Myth #2 Strive for symmetry when selecting and placing furniture, accessories, and artwork.

Myth #3 Don't mix silver and gold, and you certainly shouldn't use either with brass or weathered/aged items.

Myth #4 Always store books in bookcases, arranged by the Dewey decimal system.

Myth #5 Dishes and silverware should be seen only in matched sets.

Myth #6 Display all your "best" items together; don't use casual or sentimental pieces in the living room.

Myth #7 Only expensive items work in formal rooms.

5 Quick Changes

to a Room *You don't have to spend tons of money and replace all your furniture to breathe new life into a room you've grown tired of. I'm not even that big on moving furniture around, as most rooms seem to do best with the "anchors" in certain spots. Instead:*

Replace heavy curtains with swagged scrim or light fabric valances.

Sew or buy new pillow covers in totally different fabrics.

Toss decorative throws over the backs of the sofa and the easy chairs.

Swap displayed objects with those in another room or with favorites you might have tucked away in a closet.

Keep major pieces of furniture in place, but switch around end tables, side chairs, or lamps.

12 Accessories I Couldn't Live Without

Often, an item that might seem inconsequential by itself is just what you need to pull together the look of a room. It doesn't even have to be something intended as a collectible. A list of my very favorite things would include:

Architectural fragments

Mirrors

Family photographs

Finials

Small vases

Antique linens

Apothecary jars

Cake plates

Throws

Candlesticks

Little decorative boxes

Scrim

8 Final Steps to Luxury Living

I think you've got the picture: I surround myself with a lot of stuff and rearrange it all the time. But on a day-in, day-out basis, this is what I consider luxury in my life:

Music — I like it in every room

Fresh flowers, branches, or grasses

Grand houseplants

Candles

Notepaper and envelopes

Bowls of fresh fruits, especially in rooms other than the kitchen

Sunlight through clean windows

A little bowl of picture hooks — just to keep my juices flowing

Acknowledgments

I wish to offer my sincere thanks to everyone who helped make this book a reality.

I will always be grateful to my maternal grandmother, the original Nell Hill, for her nurturing. I still marvel at her pioneering spirit — just imagine, she crossed several states in a covered wagon! The memories of her incomparable and lovingly prepared fried chicken and lemon meringue pie nourish my soul to this day.

I owe a special debt of thanks to my parents, George and Mary Lou Diebolt, for instilling in me a love of all things retail. My favorite childhood games were not playing with dolls or blocks but pretending to have my own shop! By the time I was in elementary school, I was working at my parents' clothing store and loving every minute of it. I am fortunate to have my mother's ongoing guidance and wonderful support from my brother and sister, Tim Diebolt and Judy Diebolt. I deeply miss my late father's advice and daily visits to the store. I owe thanks also to my mother-in-law, Marguerite Garrity, who always inspires me.

Jean Lowe at Andrews McMeel Publishing in Kansas City, along with staff members Tracy Bennett, Polly Blair, Delsie Chambon, Stephanie Farley, Becky Kanning, Elizabeth Nuelle, and Marti Petty, got the ball rolling for this book and delivered us to the professional care of Smallwood & Stewart in New York City. Many thanks to their creative team of Bruce Shostak and Alexis Siroc and photographer Bryan McCay for their infinite patience and to writer Mary Caldwell for getting my story down on paper.

Several dear friends opened their homes to our photographer so we could bring to our readers an array of wonderful decorating ideas and styles. Thanks go to Marilyn and John Buehler, Brenda and Reed Graves, and Ann and Guy Humphreys.

I offer my sincerest appreciation for the fabulous day-in, day-out efforts of my right hand, Cyreesa Windsor, and the rest of the team at Nell Hill's:

Asher & Lackey Painting, Rani Bassi, Marcee Bates, Debbie Beagle, George Bilimek, Stephanie Bottiger, Jennie Buehler, Carolyn Campbell, Megan Chapin, Sharon Clayton, Jason Cline, Shirley Cline, Ashly Coder, Joyce Colman, Chubby Darrenkamp, Mary Davis, Joe Domann, Carolyn Dunn, Barb Fricke, Erin Fricke, Jane Graves, Judy Green, Lindsay Hanf, Gail Hanson, Aleda Haug, Vicki Hinde, Jo Hines, Zachary Hoyt, Emma Lou Hull, Pamela Hull, Virginia Jones, Kastens Plumbing & Heating, Dillon Kinsman, Amber Kuhnert, Nicole Liggett, Ardena Loch, June Lynn, Casey Marlatt, Megan Marlatt, Rhonda McDermed, Shannon Mize, Jeanne Mueller, Angela Mullins, Theresa Murphy, Gloria Nash, Marissa Nash, Lois Niemann, Sara Nolting, Cheryl Owens, Heather Owens, Pickman Electric, Emily Rogers, Adam Royer, John Shackelford, Corby Shields, Kathy Sledd, Angela Stuebs, Diane Sudhoff, Tate Plumbing & Construction, Chuck Tilton, Toews Construction, Kerri Wagner, Geri Weishaar, Marcellini Weishaar, Laurie Wilson, and Averie Windsor. Thanks also to our many friends and customers from Atchison, St. Joseph, Kansas City, and beyond. You are all terrific, and without you there would be no store to write about.

Finally, saving the best for last, I give my deepest thanks and love always to those dearest to my heart, Dan Garrity and Kelly Garrity.

M. C. G.